Many colorful creatures live in the cold water off a rocky coast.

Exploring the
Seashore

by William H. Amos

BOOKS FOR YOUNG EXPLORERS
NATIONAL GEOGRAPHIC SOCIETY

What will Alyssa and James find at the rocky seashore? Their guide has pulled a small creature from a pool in the rocks. The children come closer to see what lives at the edge of the ocean.

FUCUS ROCKWEED

ROCK BARNACLES, SHOWN ALMOST LIFE-SIZE

Whoosh! White with foam, waves crash against a rocky shore. Snails glide over the wet rocks, eating small plants.

Seaweeds growing on the rocks move with the water. Some have little floats at the tips of their branches. Out of water, seaweeds lie flat like a slippery blanket.

Animals have ways of staying in place as waves pound the shore. Barnacles glue themselves to rocks for life. An animal called a chiton holds on tightly, using a foot under its shell.

CHITONS (kīt-ns), SHOWN ALMOST LIFE-SIZE

PERIWINKLE SNAILS, UP TO 1 INCH LONG

Dipping their nets into a tide pool, James and Alyssa discover a small world of living creatures. James gently holds a little crab.

Twice a day water rises and falls along the shore. These changes of water level are called tides. At high tide, waves flow over the rocks, filling spaces between them. At low tide, waves do not reach the pools, but water has been left behind.

Tony Chen

MONTAGUE'S SHRIMP, UP TO 3¾ INCHES LONG

SEA STARS, ABOUT 8 INCHES ACROSS

CLAM WORM, ABOUT 4 INCHES LONG

*L*ook quietly for the animals in a tide pool. Sea peaches squirt out water if you touch them. You can see right through this shrimp. Can you find the sea stars with five arms?

A clam worm has many leglike paddles. It usually stays out of sight.

SEA PEACHES, ABOUT 3 INCHES ACROSS

A tiny hermit crab peeks out of a shell no longer than your little finger. Hermit crabs do not have shells of their own. They live in shells left by other animals.

STRAWBERRY ANEMONE (anem-o-nē)

Do you know what happens if you touch an anemone? The animal closes its arms, called tentacles, and looks like a ball. A strawberry anemone is as big as a grapefruit.

An animal called a hydroid catches food with its tentacles. It looks like a dandelion.

Sea urchins eat small plants growing on the rocks. Urchins are covered with long, sharp spines that help them move.

James and Alyssa dig through the grass in a salt marsh. Protected from the open sea, thick grasses carpet the shore. Seawater floods the marsh at high tide. At low tide, there is a lot to see on the muddy bottom.

DIAMONDBACK TERRAPIN

DIAMONDBACK TERRAPIN

GLASSWORT

Many kinds of animals and plants live in salt marshes.
Holding its head high, a turtle crawls in the mud.
A waxy-looking plant called glasswort is turning
from green to red. This tells you autumn is coming.

While the tide is out, mussels lie closed on the mud.
Their many strong threads are attached to the grass.
The threads keep the mussels from washing away.
A mussel shell has two parts. The mussel will open
its shell to feed when the tide comes in.

RIBBED MUSSELS

Fiddler crabs find food in the mud at low tide.
When the water rises, they race into their holes.
Fiddlers are about as big as they look on this page.

The male fiddler shows off for the females
by waving his large claw.

The salt marsh has food for many creatures. A muskrat nibbles on grass. Muskrats live near fresh water and in salt marshes.

Small animals may become meals for larger animals. A snowy egret is trying to catch a fish. At home in the marsh, a clapper rail sits on her nest. She eats fiddler crabs, snails, insects, and seeds.

W‌aves curl along the shore,
leaving watermarks on the sand.
The beach is always changing as
wind and water move the sand.

Waves bring in shells, seaweed,
driftwood, and many other things.
The children and their guide
gather empty shells. Behind them,
a wave rolls in with new treasures.
The sand is full of bits and pieces.

CAPE HATTERAS LIGHTHOUSE

Many creatures find a home or a meal on sandy shores. Some live in the sand at the edge of the beach. Some feed where the waves move back and forth. Others build nests in the sand dunes. Birds circle overhead, looking for food.

Tony Chen

Match the numbers on the painting with the numbers and names below.

1. razor clam	6. sandpiper	10. empty shells	15. laughing gull
2. lugworm	7. brown pelican	11. sea star	16. hognose snake
3. sand dollar	8. blue crab	12. seaweed	17. cottontail rabbit
4. mole crab	9. horseshoe crab	13. ghost crab	18. meadow vole
5. coquina	shell	14. herring gull	19. black skimmer

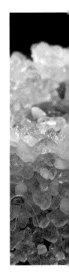

Racing a wave, young sanderlings run across the wet sand. They will catch shellfish that wash in and out with the waves.

A beach flea digs in the sand. It lives near the high-tide mark. This tiny creature usually comes out at night. It hops about, looking for food. In shallow water, a moon snail glides over the sandy bottom. Its body looks like a skirt around the shell. The snail can protect itself by pulling into its hard shell.

BEACH FLEA, UP TO 1 INCH LONG

MOON SNAIL, UP TO 3¾ INCHES ACROSS

$\mathcal{A}$bove the beach, tall grasses help build dunes. The grass has deep roots that hold the sand in place. Sand blown by the wind collects around the stems.

Alyssa feels how strong the roots of a goldenrod plant are. She is careful not to pull it out. Only a few kinds of plants grow in the dunes. The sand is often hot and dry, and the wind carries salt spray. We need to protect plants that live there.

Beach peas in a pod look like peas from a garden, but you should not eat them.

A family of gulls rests in the dunes. Most animals seek shelter while the sand is very hot. They move about in the early morning, late afternoon, or at night.

Curving its body, a black racer crawls quickly. You can follow the trail of a cricket. Its feet leave scratches in the sand.

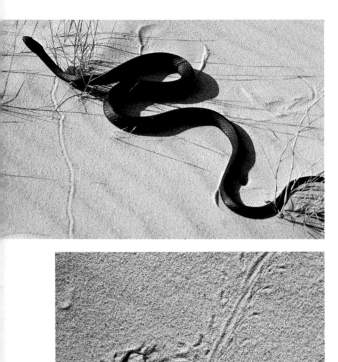

Alyssa and James empty their shoes after a day at the beach. As you explore different seashores, what will you find living where the land meets the sea?

Published by The National Geographic Society
Gilbert M. Grosvenor, *President*
Melvin M. Payne, *Chairman of the Board*
Owen R. Anderson, *Executive Vice President*
Robert L. Breeden, *Vice President, Publications and Educational Media*

Prepared by The Special Publications Division
Donald J. Crump, *Director*
Philip B. Silcott, *Associate Director*
William L. Allen, *Assistant Director*

Staff for this book
Jane H. Buxton, *Managing Editor*
Alison Wilbur Eskildsen, *Picture Editor*
Marianne R. Koszorus, *Art Director*
Brooke Jennings Kane, Elizabeth W. Fisher, *Researchers*
Carol Rocheleau Curtis, *Illustrations Assistant*
Nancy F. Berry, Dianne T. Craven, Mary Elizabeth Davis, Rosamund
Garner, Cleo Petroff, Sheryl A. Prohovich, Kathleen T. Shea,
Nancy E. Simson, Pamela Black Townsend, Linda L. Whittington,
Virginia A. Williams, *Staff Assistants*

Engraving, Printing, and Product Manufacture
Robert W. Messer, *Manager*
George V. White, *Production Manager*
George J. Zeller, Jr., *Production Project Manager*
Mark R. Dunlevy, David V. Showers, Gregory Storer,
Assistant Production Managers; Mary A. Bennett, *Production Assistant;*
Julia F. Warner, *Production Staff Assistant*

Consultants
Lynda Ehrlich, *Reading Consultant*
Lila Bishop, *Educational Consultant*
Prentice K. Stout, Marine Advisory Service, University of
Rhode Island, Narragansett, *Scientific Consultant*

Illustrations Credits
National Geographic Photographer Joseph H. Bailey (cover, 2-3, 5, 6, 7 upper,
14-15, 21 upper, 26 lower, 27, 30-31); Fred Bavendam (1, 8 upper); Robert
Mitchell (4 upper); William H. Amos (4 center, 24-25 lower); Jeff Foott (4 lower, 8
lower, 15 lower, 32); Tony Chen (7 lower, 22-23); Michael Fogden/Oxford Scientific Films (8 center); Fred Bavendam/Peter Arnold, Inc. (8-9, 13 upper, 28-29);
Alex Kerstitch (10-11); Jeff Rotman (12 upper, 12-13); ANIMALS ANIMALS/Anne
Wertheim (13 lower); Jack Dermid (15 upper left, 16-17, 19 upper and lower
right, 21 lower, 25 lower right, 28 upper and lower left); C. C. Lockwood (15
upper right); Harry Engels/PHOTO RESEARCHERS, INC./NATIONAL AUDUBON SOCI-
ETY COLLECTION (18-19); National Geographic Photographer David Alan Harvey
(20); National Geographic Photographer James P. Blair (24-25 upper); EARTH
SCENES/Patti Murray (26 upper).

The Special Publications Division is grateful for the cooperation of Alyssa
Sullivan, James Callaghan, and Prentice K. Stout, who are pictured in this book.

Library of Congress CIP Data

Amos, William Hopkins.
  Exploring the seashore.

  (Books for young explorers)
  Summary: Guided by a marine biologist, two young children examine some of the
  many forms of life found along rocky and sandy shorelines and in salt marshes
  of North America.
  1. Seashore biology—Juvenile literature. [1. Seashore biology] I. Title. II. Title:
  Seashore. III. Series.
  QH95.7.A46   1984   574.909'46   84-11464
  ISBN 0-87044-526-X (regular edition)
  ISBN 0-87044-531-6 (library edition)

Against the setting sun, a shorebird wades at the edge of the ocean.
Migrating birds often stop to rest and feed on sandy beaches.
Cover: Alyssa and James look into a tide pool on a Rhode Island shore.